AMERICAN POETS PROJECT

IS PUBLISHED WITH A GIFT IN MEMORY OF

James Merrill

AND SUPPORT FROM ITS FOUNDING PATRONS

Sidney J. Weinberg, Jr. Foundation

The Berkley Foundation

Richard B. Fisher and Jeanne Donovan Fisher

Stephen Crane

COMPLETE POEMS —

EDITED BY
CHRISTOPHER BENFEY

AMERICAN POETS PROJECT

THE LIBRARY OF AMERICA

"Uncollected Poems" reprinted from the University of Virginia Edition of *Poems and Literary Remains*. Vol. X, *The Works of Stephen Crane*, edited by Fredson Bowers. Copyright © 1975 by the Rector and Visitors of the University of Virginia.

The paper used in this publication meets the minimum requirements of the American National Standard for Information Sciences—Permanence of Paper for Printed Library Materials, ANSI Z39.48—1984.

Design by Chip Kidd and Mark Melnick.
Frontispiece reprinted courtesy of Patrick Simonelli, www.stephencrane.org.
Illustrations in *War Is Kind* courtesy of Yale Collection of American Literature, Beinecke Rare Book and Manuscript Library, Yale University.

Library of Congress Control Number: 2010942538
ISBN 978-1-59853-093-3
American Poets Project—31

First Printing

CONTENTS

War Is Kind (1899)

INTRODUCTION

1

During the severe and blizzard-ridden winter of 1894, when he managed to write some of his most distinctive work in prose and verse, Stephen Crane was a twenty-two-year-old newspaper reporter living hand to mouth in New York City. "Of all human lots for a person of sensibility," he wrote of this decisive period in his short life, "that of an obscure free lance in literature or journalism is, I think, the most discouraging." Crane's principal residence at the time, more flophouse than boarding house, was the old Art Students League building on East 23rd Street, where he shared a large studio with three artist friends. Crane wrote a vivid tribute to the building itself, an abandoned labyrinth of studios, hallways, and staircases, after the League moved uptown to its present location opposite Carnegie Hall. His description is also a suggestive evocation of his own creative mood, a sort of solitary bonhomie, at the time:

> This staid puritanical old building once contained about all that was real in the Bohemian quality of New York. The exterior belies the interior in a tremendous

degree. It is plastered with signs, and wears sedately the air of being what it is not. The interior however is a place of slumberous corridors rambling in puzzling turns and curves. The large studios rear their brown rafters over scenes of lonely quiet.

"In the top-most and remotest studio," he added, "there is an old beam which bears this line from Emerson [in his essay "Heroism"] in half-obliterated chalk marks: 'Congratulate yourselves if you have done something strange and extravagant and broken the monotony of a decorous age.'"

During those frigid months, Crane was trying to do "something strange and extravagant" on at least three different fronts. First, he was turning out vivid, highly impressionistic sketches for New York newspapers, mainly about the privations of the urban poor after the Panic of 1893 had swollen the ranks of the homeless and unemployed; second, he was finishing the manuscript of *The Red Badge of Courage*, his episodic novel of a bewildered private caught up in the chaos of the Civil War; and third, he was writing, in a white heat of creative intensity from January to March, the sixty or so short poems that eventually made up his book *The Black Riders and Other Lines*. "This winter fixes me firmly," he wrote proudly of the two books soon to be published, the *Red Badge* and *Black Riders*. "One, I think, will make an awful howl." He meant his little book of poetry.

Black Riders, which appeared in May 1895, was certainly an attention-grabbing book. The cover was graced with a swooping orchid, front and back, contributed by one of Crane's fellow residents in the Art Students League building. The pages inside were of a contrasting austerity. The "lines" were printed high up on the page, entirely in capital letters, as though they were newspaper headlines, or perhaps urgent messages telegraphed from the battle front, as in the opening of the title poem:

> BLACK RIDERS CAME FROM THE SEA.
> THERE WAS CLANG AND CLANG OF SPEAR
>   AND SHIELD,
> AND CLASH AND CLASH OF HOOF AND
>   HEEL . . .

The sixty-seven concise, untitled poems that followed were mainly of a plainspoken simplicity that matched the page design, offering observations about Truth, Nature, and God, whose death was announced in the final three entries in the book, and first broached as a question:

> If I should cast off this tattered coat,
> And go free into the mighty sky;
> If I should find nothing there
> But a vast blue,
> Echoless, ignorant,—
> What then?

Among the most memorable poems in the collection were blunt parables in verse about men performing actions either inscrutable (eating their own hearts or defying the universe) or incongruous (reading the newspaper on a mountaintop).

The contents and the design of the book had been worked out, with minor misunderstandings on both sides, between Crane and the Boston firm of Copeland and Day, who had promised something "more severely classic than any book ever yet issued in America." The arresting page design was entirely the idea of the publishers, who were aligned with the anti-industrial Arts and Crafts movement of the turn of the century. Crane's "rough-hewn" avoidance of rhyme and regular meter and his occasional medievalizing touches (as in the poem "A youth in apparel that glittered") appealed to such tendencies. Fred Holland Day, the chief financial backer of the enterprise, was a man of staggering eccentricity. A significant figure in the history of photography and the mentor of Khalil Gibran, he is perhaps best known for the soft-focus series in which he portrayed the last days of Christ, with himself in the starring role. It is easy to see why Day's firm was drawn to Crane's somewhat "Orphic" poems, as William Dean Howells described them.

Crane was delighted with the design of the book, even as the first negative reviews came in. "I see they have been pounding the wide margins, the capitals and all that but I think it great," he wrote to his publishers. After the overnight success of *The Red Badge of Courage*, which made him a famous writer in America and England, Crane continued to express his preference for his poetry. "Personally, I like my little book of poems, 'The Black Riders,' better than I do 'The Red Badge of Courage,'" he wrote. "The reason is, I suppose, that the former is the more ambitious effort. In it I aim to give my ideas of life as a whole, so far as I know it, and the latter is a mere episode,—an amplification." Controversy surrounding the book, which quickly inspired at least a hundred parodies, made it one of Copeland and Day's most successful commercial ventures.

The stir attracted the attention of Elbert Hubbard, another self-styled eccentric and Arts and Crafts proponent, who, from his base outside of Buffalo, ran a community of craftsmen and a publishing firm collectively known as the Roycrofters ("craftsmen to the king"), modeled on William Morris's Kelmscott initiative but with less attention accorded to fine craftsmanship. Hubbard's main talent was in mass-marketing; he was a pioneer in direct mail.

Among his productions was a little magazine named, with false modesty, *The Philistine*, and it was in its pages that Crane, following the appearance of *Black Riders*, published many of his remaining poems, along with such unclassifiable productions as his Beckett-like playlet "A Prologue," which Hubbard printed in caps. Many of these poems were collected in Crane's second and last volume of verse, *War Is Kind*, a more miscellaneous compilation than the unified *Black Riders*. It was published in 1899, while Crane— during a sparsely documented period in his life, when he seemed in flight from everything—was unwell and living in Havana. He died of tuberculosis the following year, at a sanatorium in the Black Forest, at the shockingly young age of twenty-eight.

2

"Art should be a child of suffering," Crane once told an editor, when thinking back to the decisive winter of 1894. For Crane, much of the suffering was self-chosen. He had aimed to lead a "life of fire," as he called it in a poem in *Black Riders*, a life that "glowed, / A dire red stain, indelible" —indelible as ink, one surmises, or blood. Episodes in his life, worthy of a pulp adventure novel, included stints as a hard-driving war reporter in Cuba and Greece; a surprisingly resilient common-law marriage to a whorehouse madam from Jacksonville; survival in a shipwreck in the Gulf of Mexico; and a brief and relatively placid country-house life in England, with friends and admiring neighbors such as Joseph Conrad and Henry James. Looking back, Crane could say that his career had been "more of a battle than a journey," encompassing poverty, war, illness, and life-threatening accident.

He was born on November 1, 1871, in Newark, New Jersey, the fourteenth and youngest child of the Reverend

Jonathan Townley Crane, who wrote tracts on the evils of urban entertainments and presided over Methodist churches in the Newark and Elizabeth districts, and Mary Helen (Peck) Crane, a temperance advocate and niece of the Methodist Bishop Jesse T. Peck. "Upon my mother's side," Crane wrote, "everybody as soon as he could walk, became a Methodist clergyman—of the old ambling-nag, saddle-bag, exhorting kind." He was prouder of the soldiers on his father's side, including his namesake, who had fought in the Revolution.

Searching for that intensity of experience dear to his own strenuous generation, Crane set his sights on a military career. After a happy sojourn at a genial military academy called Claverack College and Hudson River Institute, which he entered at sixteen, Crane briefly attended Lafayette College and Syracuse University, taking baseball more seriously than his classes. Persuaded by one of his brothers that the United States was unlikely to fight a war during his lifetime, Crane considered first mining engineering and then, while serving as a stringer for the *New York Tribune*, found in journalism some of the dangerous exposure he had hoped to find in battle. He found as well an alternative language to the literature he had studied (earning his only grade, an "A") in his otherwise desultory academic career at Syracuse. By the fall of 1891 he was done with formal education—"I had, first of all, to recover from college," he claimed. With funds inherited after the death of his mother, he published his first novel, *Maggie: A Girl of the Streets*, in 1893, an affecting portrait of a factory girl turned prostitute, and wandered the rough neighborhoods of lower Manhattan in search of further material.

In late February, he spent the night outside in a blizzard, recording—and experiencing—how the homeless people of the city responded to "gusts of snow that came down" and "cut like knives and needles." On another occasion, dressed in rags for what he called "An Experiment in Misery," he joined homeless drifters, including one he described as resembling "an assassin steeped in crimes performed awkwardly," in a public shelter. Soon after, he descended into a Pennsylvania coal mine. "Great and mystically dreadful is the earth from a mine's depth," he observed. "Man is in the implacable grasp of nature."

One might think that writing for newspapers, with their strict stylistic limitations, their word limits, and their schematic formats, would be an unlikely place for the nurturing of distinctive literary voices. In one of the poems in *The Black Riders*, Crane staged this ironic encounter between "old" and "new" wisdom:

> In a lonely place,
> I encountered a sage
> Who sat, all still,
> Regarding a newspaper.
> He accosted me:
> "Sir, what is this?"
> Then I saw that I was greater,
> Aye, greater than this sage.
> I answered him at once,
> "Old, old man, it is the wisdom of the age."
> The sage looked upon me with admiration.

But literature advances by repudiating what previous generations of writers considered "literary" or "poetic." Some of the boldest, most revolutionary innovations in American literary style, from Whitman's *Leaves of Grass* to Hemingway's *In Our Time*, have come from newspapermen. Crane's training in the intense world of the 1890s American newspaper gave him, as it had given Whitman, an alternative and more earthbound sound to the experience of daily life than that found in self-consciously literary works, and a way out of the stylistic impasse of poets of the previous generation.

As for more conventional sources for Crane's poetry, there is little agreement and sparse evidence. Hamlin Garland, the Midwestern realist who championed Crane's novels during his lifetime, was impressed when Crane told him that he could "turn the poetic spout on or off," and had unwritten poems lined up in his head "all in a little row . . . That's the way they come—in little rows, all ready to be put down on paper." In Garland's judgment, the poems "suggested some of the French translations of Japanese verses, at other times they carried the sting and compression of Emily Dickinson's verse and the savage philosophy of Olive Schreiner." Crane mentioned his admiration for Schreiner to his artist friend Corwin Linson, but any influence of her allegorical *Dreams* is remote at best. There is no convincing evidence that Crane knew Dickinson's work; the rumor that Howells had introduced her work to Crane seems wishful at best. No one has pursued, as far as I know, the suggestive link to Japanese verse in translation, at a time when versions by Judith Gautier began to make their way into English. If there were, indeed, "influences" from such diverse sources, Crane did his best to conceal them. One can say with more confidence that Crane's spare narratives in verse owe something to Jesus's parables, and the bleak landscape and bleaker moral of Shelley's "Ozymandias" seem in the background of many of them.

3

In his public pronouncements about his own work around 1894, Crane often adopts a resolutely "anti-poetic" stance. He lampooned the traditional prosody and reassuring sentiments of Longfellow's "A Psalm of Life" in a blistering, stuttering quatrain:

> Tell me not in joyous numbers
> We can make our lives sublime
> By—well, at least, not by
> Dabbling much in rhyme.

Crane told Nellie Crouse, a young woman he pursued in late 1895, that he was "very properly enraged at the word 'poet' which continually reminds me of long-hair and seems to me to be a most detestable form of insult." Of his "lines" in *Black Riders*, he insisted that "I never call them poems myself." On occasion he called them "pills," as though they were harsh medicine rather than sweet candy. "I like it," says the man eating his heart in one of Crane's best-known parables, "because it is bitter, and because it is my heart."

Crane's aim in *The Black Riders* is often to identify the truth about human existence as he conceives it, a truth that is difficult and austere, and rescue it from what he perceives to be competing and overly facile versions of it. Truth, a traveler learns in *Black Riders*, is more like "a breath, a wind," than the "mighty fortress" of the hymn. (Elizabeth Bishop's "At the Fishhouses" quotes the same hymn and concludes with the same insight about the fleeting nature of truth.) The pathway to truth, a wayfarer discovers in a poem included in *War Is Kind*, is "thickly grown with weeds." When he blithely decides to follow it, like Robert Frost's traveler faced with two diverging roads, he discovers that "each weed / Was a singular knife"; he consoles himself with the thought that "Doubtless there are other roads."

These other roads include religious hypocrisy, a frequent target in *Black Riders*, with its concomitant theme, so pervasive in Hawthorne, of "secret sin." "You say you are holy," says the speaker in one poem, "but there are those / Who see you sin, my friend." The "chief man" in another poem, leading a "white procession" in a great cathedral, is seen to "cringe / As in a place of danger," like Hawthorne's

III

IN THE DESERT
I SAW A CREATURE, NAKED, BESTIAL,
WHO, SQUATTING UPON THE GROUND,
HELD HIS HEART IN HIS HANDS,
AND ATE OF IT.
I SAID, "IS IT GOOD, FRIEND?"
"IT IS BITTER — BITTER," HE ANSWERED;
"BUT I LIKE IT
"BECAUSE IT IS BITTER,
"AND BECAUSE IT IS MY HEART."

3

A page from the first edition of *The Black Riders* (1895)

shuddering minister behind his enigmatic black veil. Standing in a "high place," Crane's speaker in yet another poem sees devils below "carousing in sin."

> One looked up, grinning,
> And I said, "Comrade! Brother!"

As Baudelaire wrote in a similar vein, "Tu le connais, lecteur, ce monstre délicat, / —Hypocrite lecteur,—mon semblable,—mon frère!" ("Reader, you know him, this delicate monster, / Hypocritical reader,—my counterpart, —my brother!")

Apparently, some of the poems Crane submitted were too religiously offensive, or otherwise unacceptable, for Copeland and Day, who refused to publish seven of them. One of these, slightly revised and included in *War Is Kind*, may be Crane's clearest artistic statement of what he was up to in his poetry:

> There was a man with tongue of wood
> Who essayed to sing,
> And in truth it was lamentable.
> But there was one who heard
> The clip-clapper of this tongue of wood
> And knew what the man
> Wished to sing,
> And with that the singer was content.

The metaphor is a bell with a wooden tongue or "clapper." The poet tries to sing like other poets, lyrically and musically, but produces a rattling "clip-clapper" sound instead. Still, there was "one who heard" what he was trying to express. The phrase "in truth it was lamentable" may conceal a double meaning: given the harshness of the times, this particular poet's "truth" can only be a "lament."

Interestingly, Zbigniew Herbert, one of that galaxy

of great poets who emerged from the successive Nazi and Soviet occupations of Poland, has a poem with a kindred theme. In "A Knocker" (as translated by Czesław Miłosz and Peter Dale Scott), Herbert invokes those facile poets "who grow / gardens in their heads" and who have only to "close their eyes" to be inundated with "schools of images." By contrast, he says,

> my imagination
> is a piece of board
> my sole instrument
> is a wooden stick

When he strikes the board, it answers him "yes—yes / no—no." This, he says, is "the moralist's dry poem." As Seamus Heaney comments, Herbert is "standing up for the down-to-earthiness of life against the flighty, carried-away fantasies of art."

Despite the parallels, there can be no serious question of influence between the two poems—unless, perhaps, Joseph Conrad, who admired Crane's writing, served as an intermediary between Crane and the Polish poets. Besides, there is an important difference. Crane's wooden-tongued man doesn't abjure lyrical singing in favor of his wooden clapper; he tries to sing and fails. And yet, both poems seem to arise from the same conviction: that the times are sufficiently bad that lyricism itself is an affront. Unlike Herbert, Crane doesn't try to imitate the lyrical music he is abjuring in "There was a man with tongue of wood." In one of his most impressive poems, however, this is precisely what he does do.

John Berryman considered Crane's opening poem to *War Is Kind* "perhaps his finest poem" and "one of the major lyrics of the century in America." The poem begins:

> Do not weep, maiden, for war is kind.
> Because your lover threw wild hands toward the sky
> And the affrighted steed ran on alone,
> Do not weep.
> War is kind.

Crane proceeds through two more addressees, babe and mother, with the same not-quite-reassuring refrain. Berryman identified two competing voices in the poem, a voice of anti-poetic "prose"—the tongue of wood—and a voice of lyrical "lament," each with its own distinctive music, down to the choice of vowels. The poem, he writes,

> is based on the letter *i* in the word "kind." There are rhymes "fie" and "lie" in the set-in stanzas; wild, sky, affrighted, flies, bright; just these, and they ought to make a high lament. But of course they do nothing of the sort. The author is standing *close* to one, not off on some platform, and the poem takes place in the successful war of the *prose* ("unexplained," "gulped," and so on) *against* the poetic appearance of lament. . . . A domestic, terrible poem, what it whispers is: "I would console you, how I would console you! *If I honestly could.*"

This is brilliantly said, and also captures something important in Berryman's own two-voiced poetry, such as his famous Dream Song 14, which begins "Life, friends, is boring." Another possible reason, perhaps unconscious, for the admiration bestowed on "Do not weep, maiden" may be the striking parallels it exhibits, in structure and specific phrasing, with Dylan Thomas's famous villanelle "Do Not Go Gentle Into that Good Night."

4

Wallace Stevens attended Stephen Crane's funeral in New York, on June 28, 1900, as a cub reporter for the *Tribune*, a paper Crane had worked for eight years earlier. For Stevens, the shock of the occasion, as he noted in his journal, was its obscurity: "the hearse rattled up the street over the cobbles, in the stifling heat of the sun, with not a single person paying the least attention to it." Crane's poetry, during the century since it first appeared, has suffered a kindred fate. Amy Lowell, in her posthumously published introduction in 1926, lamented "the thirty-year neglect" of Crane's poems. Thirty years later, in the only sustained monograph on Crane's poetry to date, Daniel Hoffman, noting the scant bibliography of critical work on Crane's poetry, maintained that "Crane's stature as a poet remains to be determined." Crane has seemed, at best, a transitional figure between major nineteenth-century poets and the rise of literary modernism; Berryman calls him "the important American poet between Walt Whitman and Emily Dickinson on one side, and his tardy-developing contemporaries Edwin Arlington Robinson and Robert Frost with Ezra Pound on the other." Nonetheless, Crane has rarely been treated as a significant poet in his own right.

What has changed during the half century since Hoffman's book is that readers today are exposed to a much wider range of verbal art recognizable as poetry. In Crane's time, the "lines" barely registered as poems at all. As sophisticated a critic as William Dean Howells, who was perfectly familiar with Whitman, wished Crane had given his lines "more form," and quipped: "I do not think a merciful Providence meant the 'prose-poem' to last." The Imagist generation of Amy Lowell and Ezra Pound could imagine that Crane's gnomic utterances meshed with their own experiments in concision and fragmentation; and yet, the harshly stated convictions about war and God in his lines had little in common with their no-ideas-but-in-things preference for indirection and suggestiveness. Perhaps the poets who might have found Crane's poetry most congenial were the traumatized veterans of World War I such as Wilfred Owen or Siegfried Sassoon, but it seems unlikely that they were familiar with anything of Crane's beyond *The Red Badge of Courage*.

During the 1950s, a prevailing neo-Symbolist aesthetic led poet-critics like John Berryman and Daniel Hoffman to overvalue poems like "Do not weep, maiden" and "The blue battalions" to the detriment of Crane's more explicit verse-parables. Even a critic as astute as Berryman could look at Crane's three-line masterpiece, a summation of the plot of his great story "The Blue Hotel,"

> A man feared that he might find an assassin;
> Another that he might find a victim.
> One was more wise than the other.

and comment, "The indifference to craft, to *how* the thing is said, is lunar." How exactly, one wonders, could the "thing" have been better said?

Two developments have rendered Crane's poetry more audible to twenty-first-century readers. One was the rise of a kind of poetry, primarily during the Sixties and early Seventies, that combined emphatic or "deep" imagery with social criticism. I am thinking of certain poems by Robert Bly, James Wright, and W. S. Merwin in response—sometimes quite obliquely and sometimes more explicitly—to the Vietnam War. Beginning during the same period, there was a rich transfusion of European and Latin American poetry via translation. Some of these poems, especially by poets of Eastern Europe such as Herbert, Czesław Miłosz, and Wisława Szymborska, share an explicitly anti-lyrical stance with Crane's lines.

Crane's poem about the man with the tongue of wood suggests that a poet needs only one sympathetic reader to be content. But there is reason to believe that Crane's lines, a long and violent century after their composition in the dilapidated Art Students League building, will eventually find their rightful audience. And when they do, it seems likely that it will be Crane's wooden-tongued verse-parables, the blunter the better, that will carry the day. "I always want to be unmistakable," Crane told one of his Syracuse fraternity brothers. "That to my mind is good writing." And Crane the poet, at his most unmistakable, sounds like this:

> A man said to the universe:
> "Sir, I exist!"
> "However," replied the universe,
> "The fact has not created in me
> "A sense of obligation."

Christopher Benfey
August 2010

THE BLACK RIDERS AND OTHER LINES

(1895)

Cover of *The Black Riders* (1895), with a design by Frederick Gordon

I

Black riders came from the sea.
There was clang and clang of spear and shield,
And clash and clash of hoof and heel,
Wild shouts and the wave of hair
In the rush upon the wind:
Thus the ride of sin.

II

Three little birds in a row
Sat musing.
A man passed near that place.
Then did the little birds nudge each other.

They said: "He thinks he can sing."
They threw back their heads to laugh.
With quaint countenances
They regarded him.
They were very curious,
Those three little birds in a row.

III

In the desert
I saw a creature, naked, bestial,
Who, squatting upon the ground,
Held his heart in his hands,
And ate of it.
I said, "Is it good, friend?"
"It is bitter—bitter," he answered;
"But I like it
"Because it is bitter,
"And because it is my heart."

IV

Yes, I have a thousand tongues,
And nine and ninety-nine lie.
Though I strive to use the one,
It will make no melody at my will,
But is dead in my mouth.

V

Once there came a man
Who said,
"Range me all men of the world in rows."
And instantly
There was terrific clamor among the people
Against being ranged in rows.
There was a loud quarrel, world-wide.
It endured for ages;
And blood was shed
By those who would not stand in rows,
And by those who pined to stand in rows.
Eventually, the man went to death, weeping.
And those who staid in bloody scuffle
Knew not the great simplicity.

VI

God fashioned the ship of the world carefully.
With the infinite skill of an all-master
Made He the hull and the sails,
Held He the rudder
Ready for adjustment.
Erect stood He, scanning His work proudly.
Then—at fateful time—a wrong called,
And God turned, heeding.
Lo, the ship, at this opportunity, slipped slyly,
Making cunning noiseless travel down the ways.
So that, forever rudderless, it went upon the seas
Going ridiculous voyages,
Making quaint progress,
Turning as with serious purpose
Before stupid winds.
And there were many in the sky
Who laughed at this thing.

VII

Mystic shadow, bending near me,
Who art thou?
Whence come ye?
And—tell me—is it fair
Or is the truth bitter as eaten fire?
Tell me!
Fear not that I should quaver,
For I dare—I dare.
Then, tell me!

VIII

I looked here;
I looked there;
Nowhere could I see my love.
And—this time—
She was in my heart.
Truly, then, I have no complaint
For though she be fair and fairer,
She is none so fair as she
In my heart.

IX

I stood upon a high place,
And saw, below, many devils
Running, leaping,
And carousing in sin.
One looked up, grinning,
And said, "Comrade! Brother!"

X

Should the wide world roll away,
Leaving black terror,
Limitless night,
Nor God, nor man, nor place to stand
Would be to me essential
If thou and thy white arms were there,
And the fall to doom a long way.

XI

In a lonely place,
I encountered a sage
Who sat, all still,
Regarding a newspaper.
He accosted me:
"Sir, what is this?"
Then I saw that I was greater,
Aye, greater than this sage.
I answered him at once,
"Old, old man, it is the wisdom of the age."
The sage looked upon me with admiration.

XII

"And the sins of the fathers shall be visited upon the heads of the children, even unto the third and fourth generation of them that hate me."

Well, then, I hate Thee, unrighteous picture;
Wicked image, I hate Thee;
So, strike with Thy vengeance
The heads of those little men
Who come blindly.
It will be a brave thing.

XIII

If there is a witness to my little life,
To my tiny throes and struggles,
He sees a fool;
And it is not fine for gods to menace fools.

XIV

There was crimson clash of war.
Lands turned black and bare;
Women wept;
Babes ran, wondering.
There came one who understood not these things.
He said, "Why is this?"
Whereupon a million strove to answer him.
There was such intricate clamor of tongues,
That still the reason was not.

XV

"Tell brave deeds of war."

Then they recounted tales,—
"There were stern stands
"And bitter runs for glory."

Ah, I think there were braver deeds.

XVI

Charity, thou art a lie,
A toy of women,
A pleasure of certain men.
In the presence of justice,
Lo, the walls of the temple
Are visible
Through thy form of sudden shadows.

XVII

There were many who went in huddled procession,
They knew not whither;
But, at any rate, success or calamity
Would attend all in equality.

There was one who sought a new road.
He went into direful thickets,
And ultimately he died thus, alone;
But they said he had courage.

XVIII

In Heaven,
Some little blades of grass
Stood before God.
"What did you do?"
Then all save one of the little blades
Began eagerly to relate
The merits of their lives.
This one stayed a small way behind,
Ashamed.
Presently, God said,
"And what did you do?"
The little blade answered, "Oh, my lord,
"Memory is bitter to me,
"For, if I did good deeds,
"I know not of them."
Then God, in all His splendor,
Arose from His throne.
"Oh, best little blade of grass!" He said.

XIX

A god in wrath
Was beating a man;
He cuffed him loudly
With thunderous blows
That rang and rolled over the earth.
All people came running.
The man screamed and struggled,
And bit madly at the feet of the god.
The people cried,
"Ah, what a wicked man!"
And—
"Ah, what a redoubtable god!"

XX

A learned man came to me once.
He said, "I know the way,—come."
And I was overjoyed at this.
Together we hastened.
Soon, too soon, were we
Where my eyes were useless,
And I knew not the ways of my feet.
I clung to the hand of my friend;
But at last he cried, "I am lost."

XXI

There was, before me,
Mile upon mile
Of snow, ice, burning sand.
And yet I could look beyond all this,
To a place of infinite beauty;
And I could see the loveliness of her
Who walked in the shade of the trees.
When I gazed,
All was lost
But this place of beauty and her.
When I gazed,
And in my gazing, desired,
Then came again
Mile upon mile,
Of snow, ice, burning sand.

XXII

Once I saw mountains angry,
And ranged in battle-front.
Against them stood a little man;
Aye, he was no bigger than my finger.
I laughed, and spoke to one near me,
"Will he prevail?"
"Surely," replied this other;
"His grandfathers beat them many times."
Then did I see much virtue in grandfathers,—
At least, for the little man
Who stood against the mountains.

XXIII

Places among the stars,
Soft gardens near the sun,
Keep your distant beauty;
Shed no beams upon my weak heart.
Since she is here
In a place of blackness,
Not your golden days
Nor your silver nights
Can call me to you.
Since she is here
In a place of blackness,
Here I stay and wait.

XXIV

I saw a man pursuing the horizon;
Round and round they sped.
I was disturbed at this;
I accosted the man.
"It is futile," I said,
"You can never—"

"You lie," he cried,
And ran on.

XXV

Behold, the grave of a wicked man,
And near it, a stern spirit.

There came a drooping maid with violets,
But the spirit grasped her arm.
"No flowers for him," he said.
The maid wept:
"Ah, I loved him."
But the spirit, grim and frowning:
"No flowers for him."

Now, this is it—
If the spirit was just,
Why did the maid weep?

XXVI

There was set before me a mighty hill,
And long days I climbed
Through regions of snow.
When I had before me the summit-view,
It seemed that my labor
Had been to see gardens
Lying at impossible distances.

XXVII

A youth in apparel that glittered
Went to walk in a grim forest.
There he met an assassin
Attired all in garb of old days;
He, scowling through the thickets,
And dagger poised quivering,
Rushed upon the youth.
"Sir," said this latter,
"I am enchanted, believe me,
"To die, thus,
"In this medieval fashion,
"According to the best legends;
"Ah, what joy!"
Then took he the wound, smiling,
And died, content.

XXVIII

"Truth," said a traveller,
"Is a rock, a mighty fortress;
"Often have I been to it,
"Even to its highest tower,
"From whence the world looks black."

"Truth," said a traveller,
"Is a breath, a wind,
"A shadow, a phantom;
"Long have I pursued it,
"But never have I touched
"The hem of its garment."

And I believed the second traveller;
For truth was to me
A breath, a wind,
A shadow, a phantom,
And never had I touched
The hem of its garment.

XXIX

Behold, from the land of the farther suns
I returned.
And I was in a reptile-swarming place,
Peopled, otherwise, with grimaces,
Shrouded above in black impenetrableness.
I shrank, loathing,
Sick with it.
And I said to him,
"What is this?"
He made answer slowly,
"Spirit, this is a world;
"This was your home."

XXX

Supposing that I should have the courage
To let a red sword of virtue
Plunge into my heart,
Letting to the weeds of the ground
My sinful blood,
What can you offer me?
A gardened castle?
A flowery kingdom?

What? A hope?
Then hence with your red sword of virtue.

XXXI

Many workmen
Built a huge ball of masonry
Upon a mountain-top.
Then they went to the valley below,
And turned to behold their work.
"It is grand," they said;
They loved the thing.

Of a sudden, it moved:
It came upon them swiftly;
It crushed them all to blood.
But some had opportunity to squeal.

XXXII

Two or three angels
Came near to the earth.
They saw a fat church.
Little black streams of people
Came and went in continually.
And the angels were puzzled
To know why the people went thus,
And why they stayed so long within.

XXXIII

There was One I met upon the road
Who looked at me with kind eyes.
He said: "Show me of your wares."
And this I did
Holding forth one.
He said: "It is a sin."
Then held I forth another.
He said: "It is a sin."
Then held I forth another.
He said: "It is a sin."
And so to the end
Always He said: "It is a sin."
And, finally, I cried out:
"But I have none other."
Then did He look at me
With kinder eyes.
"Poor soul," He said.

XXXIV

I stood upon a highway,
And, behold, there came
Many strange pedlers.
To me each one made gestures,
Holding forth little images, saying,
"This is my pattern of God.
"Now this is the God I prefer."

But I said, "Hence!
"Leave me with mine own,
"And take you yours away;
"I can't buy of your patterns of God,
"The little gods you may rightly prefer."

XXXV

A man saw a ball of gold in the sky;
He climbed for it,
And eventually he achieved it—
It was clay.

Now this is the strange part:
When the man went to the earth
And looked again,
Lo, there was the ball of gold.
Now this is the strange part:
It was a ball of gold.
Aye, by the heavens, it was a ball of gold.

XXXVI

I met a seer.
He held in his hands
The book of wisdom.
"Sir," I addressed him,
"Let me read."
"Child—" he began.
"Sir," I said,
"Think not that I am a child,
"For already I know much
"Of that which you hold.
"Aye, much."

He smiled.
Then he opened the book
And held it before me.—
Strange that I should have grown so suddenly blind.

XXXVII

On the horizon the peaks assembled;
And as I looked,
The march of the mountains began.
As they marched, they sang,
"Aye! We come! We come!"

XXXVIII

The ocean said to me once,
"Look!
"Yonder on the shore
"Is a woman, weeping.
"I have watched her.
"Go you and tell her this,—
"Her lover I have laid
"In cool green hall.
"There is wealth of golden sand
"And pillars, coral-red;
"Two white fish stand guard at his bier.

"Tell her this
"And more,—
"That the king of the seas
"Weeps too, old, helpless man.
"The bustling fates
"Heap his hands with corpses
"Until he stands like a child
"With surplus of toys."

XXXIX

The livid lightnings flashed in the clouds;
The leaden thunders crashed.
A worshipper raised his arm.
"Hearken! Hearken! The voice of God!"

"Not so," said a man.
"The voice of God whispers in the heart
"So softly
"That the soul pauses,
"Making no noise,
"And strives for these melodies,
"Distant, sighing, like faintest breath,
"And all the being is still to hear."

XL

And you love me?

I love you.

You are, then, cold coward.

Aye; but, beloved,
When I strive to come to you,
Man's opinions, a thousand thickets,
My interwoven existence,
My life,
Caught in the stubble of the world
Like a tender veil,—
This stays me.
No strange move can I make
Without noise of tearing.
I dare not.

If love loves,
There is no world
Nor word.
All is lost
Save thought of love
And place to dream.
You love me?

I love you.

You are, then, cold coward.

Aye; but, beloved—

XLI

Love walked alone.
The rocks cut her tender feet,
And the brambles tore her fair limbs.
There came a companion to her,
But, alas, he was no help,
For his name was Heart's Pain.

XLII

I walked in a desert.
And I cried,
"Ah, God, take me from this place!"
A voice said, "It is no desert."
I cried, "Well, but—
"The sand, the heat, the vacant horizon."
A voice said, "It is no desert."

XLIII

There came whisperings in the winds:
"Good-bye! Good-bye!"
Little voices called in the darkness:
"Good-bye! Good-bye!"
Then I stretched forth my arms.
"No— No—"
There came whisperings in the wind:
"Good-bye! Good-bye!"
Little voices called in the darkness:
"Good-bye! Good-bye!"

XLIV

I was in the darkness;
I could not see my words
Nor the wishes of my heart.
Then suddenly there was a great light—

"Let me into the darkness again."

XLV

Tradition, thou art for suckling children,
Thou art the enlivening milk for babes;
But no meat for men is in thee.
Then—
But, alas, we all are babes.

XLVI

Many red devils ran from my heart
And out upon the page.
They were so tiny
The pen could mash them.
And many struggled in the ink.
It was strange
To write in this red muck
Of things from my heart.

XLVII

"Think as I think," said a man,
"Or you are abominably wicked;
"You are a toad."

And after I had thought of it,
I said, "I will, then, be a toad."

XLVIII

Once there was a man,—
Oh, so wise!
In all drink
He detected the bitter,
And in all touch
He found the sting.
At last he cried thus:
"There is nothing,—
"No life,
"No joy,
"No pain,—
"There is nothing save opinion,
"And opinion be damned."

XLIX

I stood musing in a black world,
Not knowing where to direct my feet.
And I saw the quick stream of men
Pouring ceaselessly,
Filled with eager faces,
A torrent of desire.
I called to them,
"Where do you go? What do you see?"
A thousand voices called to me.
A thousand fingers pointed.
"Look! Look! There!"

I know not of it.
But, lo! in the far sky shone a radiance
Ineffable, divine,—
A vision painted upon a pall;
And sometimes it was,
And sometimes it was not.
I hesitated.
Then from the stream
Came roaring voices,
Impatient:
"Look! Look! There!"

So again I saw,
And leaped, unhesitant,
And struggled and fumed

With outspread clutching fingers.
The hard hills tore my flesh;
The ways bit my feet.
At last I looked again.

No radiance in the far sky,
Ineffable, divine;
No vision painted upon a pall;
And always my eyes ached for the light.
Then I cried in despair,
"I see nothing! Oh, where do I go?"
The torrent turned again its faces:
"Look! Look! There!"

And at the blindness of my spirit
They screamed,
"Fool! Fool! Fool!"

L

You say you are holy,
And that
Because I have not seen you sin.
Aye, but there are those
Who see you sin, my friend.

LI

A man went before a strange god,—
The god of many men, sadly wise.
And the deity thundered loudly,
Fat with rage, and puffing,
"Kneel, mortal, and cringe
"And grovel and do homage
"To my particularly sublime majesty."

The man fled.

Then the man went to another god,—
The god of his inner thoughts.
And this one looked at him
With soft eyes
Lit with infinite comprehension,
And said, "My poor child!"

LII

Why do you strive for greatness, fool?
Go pluck a bough and wear it.
It is as sufficing.

My lord, there are certain barbarians
Who tilt their noses
As if the stars were flowers,
And thy servant is lost among their shoe-buckles.
Fain would I have mine eyes even with their eyes.

Fool, go pluck a bough and wear it.

LIII

I

Blustering god,
Stamping across the sky
With loud swagger,
I fear you not.
No, though from your highest heaven
You plunge your spear at my heart,
I fear you not.
No, not if the blow
Is as the lightning blasting a tree,
I fear you not, puffing braggart.

II

If thou can see into my heart
That I fear thee not,
Thou wilt see why I fear thee not,
And why it is right.
So threaten not, thou, with thy bloody spears,
Else thy sublime ears shall hear curses.

III

Withal, there is one whom I fear;
I fear to see grief upon that face.
Perchance, friend, he is not your god;
If so, spit upon him.
By it you will do no profanity.
But I—
Ah, sooner would I die
Than see tears in those eyes of my soul.

LIV

"It was wrong to do this," said the angel.
"You should live like a flower,
"Holding malice like a puppy,
"Waging war like a lambkin."

"Not so," quoth the man
Who had no fear of spirits;
"It is only wrong for angels
"Who can live like the flowers,
"Holding malice like the puppies,
"Waging war like the lambkins."

LV

A man toiled on a burning road,
Never resting.
Once he saw a fat, stupid ass
Grinning at him from a green place.
The man cried out in rage,
"Ah! do not deride me, fool!
"I know you—
"All day stuffing your belly,
"Burying your heart
"In grass and tender sprouts:
"It will not suffice you."
But the ass only grinned at him from the green place.

LVI

A man feared that he might find an assassin;
Another that he might find a victim.
One was more wise than the other.

LVII

With eye and with gesture
You say you are holy.
I say you lie;
For I did see you
Draw away your coats
From the sin upon the hands
Of a little child.
Liar!

LVIII

The sage lectured brilliantly.
Before him, two images:
"Now this one is a devil,
"And this one is me."
He turned away.
Then a cunning pupil
Changed the positions.
Turned the sage again:
"Now this one is a devil,
"And this one is me."
The pupils sat, all grinning,
And rejoiced in the game.
But the sage was a sage.

LIX

Walking in the sky,
A man in strange black garb
Encountered a radiant form.
Then his steps were eager;
Bowed he devoutly.
"My lord," said he.
But the spirit knew him not.

LX

Upon the road of my life,
Passed me many fair creatures,
Clothed all in white, and radiant.
To one, finally, I made speech:
"Who art thou?"
But she, like the others,
Kept cowled her face,
And answered in haste, anxiously,
"I am Good Deed, forsooth;
"You have often seen me."
"Not uncowled," I made reply.
And with rash and strong hand,
Though she resisted,
I drew away the veil
And gazed at the features of Vanity.
She, shamefaced, went on;
And after I had mused a time,
I said of myself,
                              "Fool!"

LXI

I

There was a man and a woman
Who sinned.
Then did the man heap the punishment
All upon the head of her,
And went away gayly.

II

There was a man and a woman
Who sinned.
And the man stood with her.
As upon her head, so upon his,
Fell blow and blow,
And all people screaming, "Fool!"
He was a brave heart.

III

He was a brave heart.
Would you speak with him, friend?
Well, he is dead,
And there went your opportunity.
Let it be your grief
That he is dead
And your opportunity gone;
For, in that, you were a coward.

LXII

There was a man who lived a life of fire.
Even upon the fabric of time,
Where purple becomes orange
And orange purple,
This life glowed,
A dire red stain, indelible;
Yet when he was dead,
He saw that he had not lived.

LXIII

There was a great cathedral.
To solemn songs,
A white procession
Moved toward the altar.
The chief man there
Was erect, and bore himself proudly.
Yet some could see him cringe,
As in a place of danger,
Throwing frightened glances into the air,
A-start at threatening faces of the past.

LXIV

Friend, your white beard sweeps the ground.
Why do you stand, expectant?
Do you hope to see it
In one of your withered days?
With your old eyes
Do you hope to see
The triumphal march of justice?
Do not wait, friend!
Take your white beard
And your old eyes
To more tender lands.

LXV

Once, I knew a fine song,
—It is true, believe me,—
It was all of birds,
And I held them in a basket;
When I opened the wicket,
Heavens! They all flew away.
I cried, "Come back, little thoughts!"
But they only laughed.
They flew on
Until they were as sand
Thrown between me and the sky.

LXVI

If I should cast off this tattered coat,
And go free into the mighty sky;
If I should find nothing there
But a vast blue,
Echoless, ignorant,—
What then?

LXVII

God lay dead in Heaven;
Angels sang the hymn of the end;
Purple winds went moaning,
Their wings drip-dripping
With blood
That fell upon the earth.
It, groaning thing,
Turned black and sank.
Then from the far caverns
Of dead sins
Came monsters, livid with desire.
They fought,
Wrangled over the world,
A morsel.
But of all sadness this was sad,—
A woman's arms tried to shield
The head of a sleeping man
From the jaws of the final beast.

LXVIII

A spirit sped
Through spaces of night;
And as he sped, he called,
"God! God!"
He went through valleys
Of black death-slime,
Ever calling,
"God! God!"
Their echoes
From crevice and cavern
Mocked him:
"God! God! God!"
Fleetly into the plains of space
He went, ever calling,
"God! God!"
Eventually, then, he screamed,
Mad in denial,
"Ah, there is no God!"
A swift hand,
A sword from the sky,
Smote him,
And he was dead.

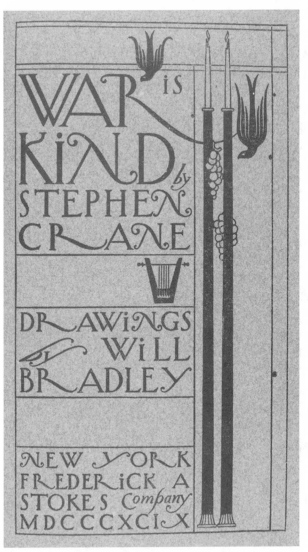

Title page of *War Is Kind* (1899)

WAR IS KIND

(1899)

———

Do not weep, maiden, for war is kind.
Because your lover threw wild hands toward the sky
And the affrighted steed ran on alone,
Do not weep.
War is kind.

Hoarse, booming drums of the regiment,
Little souls who thirst for fight,
These men were born to drill and die.
The unexplained glory flies above them,
Great is the battle-god, great, and his kingdom—
A field where a thousand corpses lie.

Do not weep, babe, for war is kind.
Because your father tumbled in the yellow trenches,
Raged at his breast, gulped and died,
Do not weep.
War is kind.

Swift blazing flag of the regiment,
Eagle with crest of red and gold,
These men were born to drill and die.
Point for them the virtue of slaughter,
Make plain to them the excellence of killing
And a field where a thousand corpses lie.

Mother whose heart hung humble as a button
On the bright splendid shroud of your son,
Do not weep.
War is kind.

———

"What says the sea, little shell?
"What says the sea?
"Long has our brother been silent to us,
"Kept his message for the ships,
"Awkward ships, stupid ships."

"The sea bids you mourn, O Pines,
"Sing low in the moonlight.
"He sends tale of the land of doom,
"Of place where endless falls
"A rain of women's tears,
"And men in grey robes—
"Men in grey robes—
"Chant the unknown pain."

"What says the sea, little shell?
"What says the sea?
"Long has our brother been silent to us,
"Kept his message for the ships,
"Puny ships, silly ships."

"The sea bids you teach, O Pines,
"Sing low in the moonlight;
"Teach the gold of patience,
"Cry gospel of gentle hands,
"Cry a brotherhood of hearts.
"The sea bids you teach, O Pines."

"And where is the reward, little shell?
"What says the sea?
"Long has our brother been silent to us,
"Kept his message for the ships,
"Puny ships, silly ships."
"No word says the sea, O Pines,
"No word says the sea.
"Long will your brother be silent to you,
"Keep his message for the ships,
"O, puny pines, silly pines."

———

To the maiden
The sea was blue meadow,
Alive with little froth-people
Singing.

To the sailor, wrecked,
The sea was dead grey walls
Superlative in vacancy,
Upon which nevertheless at fateful time,
Was written
The grim hatred of nature.

—

A little ink more or less!
It surely can't matter?
Even the sky and the opulent sea,
The plains and the hills, aloof,
Hear the uproar of all these books.
But it is only a little ink more or less.

What?
You define me God with these trinkets?
Can my misery meal on an ordered walking
Of surpliced numskulls?
And a fanfare of lights?
Or even upon the measured pulpitings
Of the familiar false and true?
Is this God?
Where, then, is hell?
Show me some bastard mushroom
Sprung from a pollution of blood.
It is better.

Where is God?

———

"Have you ever made a just man?"
"Oh, I have made three," answered God,
"But two of them are dead,
"And the third—
"Listen! Listen!
"And you will hear the thud of his defeat."

———

I explain the silvered passing of a ship at night,
The sweep of each sad lost wave,
The dwindling boom of the steel thing's striving,
The little cry of a man to a man,
A shadow falling across the greyer night,
And the sinking of the small star;

Then the waste, the far waste of waters,
And the soft lashing of black waves
For long and in loneliness.

Remember, thou, O ship of love,
Thou leavest a far waste of waters,
And the soft lashing of black waves
For long and in loneliness.

———

"I have heard the sunset song of the birches,
"A white melody in the silence,
"I have seen a quarrel of the pines.
"At nightfall
"The little grasses have rushed by me
"With the wind men.
"These things have I lived," quoth the maniac,
"Possessing only eyes and ears.
"But you—
"You don green spectacles before you look at roses."

Fast rode the knight
With spurs, hot and reeking,
Ever waving an eager sword.
"To save my lady!"
Fast rode the knight,
And leaped from saddle to war.
Men of steel flickered and gleamed
Like riot of silver lights,
And the gold of the knight's good banner
Still waved on a castle wall.

*   *   *

A horse,
Blowing, staggering, bloody thing
Forgotten at foot of castle wall.
A horse
Dead at foot of castle wall.

———

Forth went the candid man
And spoke freely to the wind—
When he looked about him he was in a far strange country.

Forth went the candid man
And spoke freely to the stars—
Yellow light tore sight from his eyes.

"My good fool," said a learned bystander,
"Your operations are mad."

"You are too candid," cried the candid man.
And when his stick left the head of the learned bystander
It was two sticks.

———

You tell me this is God?
I tell you this is a printed list,
A burning candle and an ass.

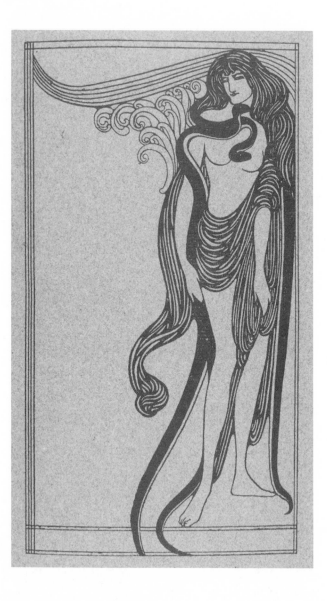

—

On the desert
A silence from the moon's deepest valley.
Fire-rays fall athwart the robes
Of hooded men, squat and dumb.
Before them, a woman
Moves to the blowing of shrill whistles
And distant-thunder of drums,
While mystic things, sinuous, dull with terrible color,
Sleepily fondle her body
Or move at her will, swishing stealthily over the sand.
The snakes whisper softly;
The whispering, whispering snakes,
Dreaming and swaying and staring,
But always whispering, softly whispering.
The wind streams from the lone reaches
Of Arabia, solemn with night,
And the wild fire makes shimmer of blood
Over the robes of the hooded men
Squat and dumb.
Bands of moving bronze, emerald, yellow,
Circle the throat and the arms of her,
And over the sands serpents move warily
Slow, menacing and submissive,
Swinging to the whistles and drums,
The whispering, whispering snakes,
Dreaming and swaying and staring,
But always whispering, softly whispering.
The dignity of the accursèd;
The glory of slavery, despair, death,
Is in the dance of the whispering snakes.

—

A newspaper is a collection of half-injustices
Which, bawled by boys from mile to mile,
Spreads its curious opinion
To a million merciful and sneering men,
While families cuddle the joys of the fireside
When spurred by tale of dire lone agony.
A newspaper is a court
Where every one is kindly and unfairly tried
By a squalor of honest men.
A newspaper is a market
Where wisdom sells its freedom
And melons are crowned by the crowd.
A newspaper is a game
Where his error scores the player victory
While another's skill wins death.
A newspaper is a symbol;
It is fetless life's chronicle,
A collection of loud tales
Concentrating eternal stupidities,
That in remote ages lived unhaltered,
Roaming through a fenceless world.

The wayfarer,
Perceiving the pathway to truth,
Was struck with astonishment.
It was thickly grown with weeds.
"Ha," he said,
"I see that none has passed here
"In a long time."
Later he saw that each weed
Was a singular knife.
"Well," he mumbled at last,
"Doubtless there are other roads."

A slant of sun on dull brown walls,
A forgotten sky of bashful blue.

Toward God a mighty hymn,
A song of collisions and cries,
Rumbling wheels, hoof-beats, bells,
Welcomes, farewells, love-calls, final moans,
Voices of joy, idiocy, warning, despair,
The unknown appeals of brutes,
The chanting of flowers,
The screams of cut trees,
The senseless babble of hens and wise men—
A cluttered incoherency that says at the stars:
"O God, save us!"

Once a man clambering to the house-tops
Appealed to the heavens.
With strong voice he called to the deaf spheres;
A warrior's shout he raised to the suns.
Lo, at last, there was a dot on the clouds,
And—at last and at last—
—God—the sky was filled with armies.

———

There was a man with tongue of wood
Who essayed to sing,
And in truth it was lamentable.
But there was one who heard
The clip-clapper of this tongue of wood
And knew what the man
Wished to sing,
And with that the singer was content.

The successful man has thrust himself
Through the water of the years,
Reeking wet with mistakes,—
Bloody mistakes;
Slimed with victories over the lesser,
A figure thankful on the shore of money.
Then, with the bones of fools
He buys silken banners
Limned with his triumphant face;
With the skins of wise men
He buys the trivial bows of all.
Flesh painted with marrow
Contributes a coverlet,
A coverlet for his contented slumber.
In guiltless ignorance, in ignorant guilt,
He delivers his secrets to the riven multitude.
    "Thus I defended: Thus I wrought."
Complacent, smiling,
He stands heavily on the dead.
Erect on a pillar of skulls
He declaims his trampling of babes;
Smirking, fat, dripping,
He makes speech in guiltless ignorance,
Innocence.

In the night
Grey heavy clouds muffled the valleys,
And the peaks looked toward God alone.
    "O Master that movest the wind with a finger,
    "Humble, idle, futile peaks are we.
    "Grant that we may run swiftly across the world
    "To huddle in worship at Thy feet."

In the morning
A noise of men at work came the clear blue miles,
And the little black cities were apparent.
    "O Master that knowest the meaning of raindrops,
    "Humble, idle, futile peaks are we.
    "Give voice to us, we pray, O Lord,
    "That we may sing Thy goodness to the sun."

In the evening
The far valleys were sprinkled with tiny lights.
    "O Master,
    "Thou that knowest the value of kings and birds,
    "Thou hast made us humble, idle, futile peaks.
    "Thou only needest eternal patience;
    "We bow to Thy wisdom, O Lord—
    "Humble, idle, futile peaks."

In the night
Grey heavy clouds muffled the valleys,
And the peaks looked toward God alone.

———

The chatter of a death-demon from a tree-top.

Blood—blood and torn grass—
Had marked the rise of his agony—
This lone hunter.
The grey-green woods impassive
Had watched the threshing of his limbs.

A canoe with flashing paddle,
A girl with soft searching eyes,
A call: "John!"

*   *   *

Come, arise, hunter!
Can you not hear?

The chatter of a death-demon from a tree-top.

The impact of a dollar upon the heart
Smiles warm red light,
Sweeping from the hearth rosily upon the white table,
With the hanging cool velvet shadows
Moving softly upon the door.

The impact of a million dollars
Is a crash of flunkys,
And yawning emblems of Persia
Cheeked against oak, France and a sabre,
The outcry of old beauty
Whored by pimping merchants
To submission before wine and chatter.
Silly rich peasants stamp the carpets of men,
Dead men who dreamed fragrance and light
Into their woof, their lives;
The rug of an honest bear
Under the feet of a cryptic slave
Who speaks always of baubles,
Forgetting state, multitude, work, and state,
Champing and mouthing of hats
Making ratful squeak of hats,
Hats.

———

A man said to the universe:
"Sir, I exist!"
"However," replied the universe,
"The fact has not created in me
"A sense of obligation."

———

When the prophet, a complacent fat man,
Arrived at the mountain-top,
He cried: "Woe to my knowledge!
"I intended to see good white lands
"And bad black lands,
"But the scene is grey."

There was a land where lived no violets.
A traveller at once demanded: "Why?"
The people told him:
"Once the violets of this place spoke thus:
"'Until some woman freely gives her lover
"'To another woman
"'We will fight in bloody scuffle.'"
Sadly the people added:
"There are no violets here."

———

There was one I met upon the road
Who looked at me with kind eyes.
He said: "Show me of your wares."
And I did,
Holding forth one.
He said: "It is a sin."
Then I held forth another.
He said: "It is a sin."
Then I held forth another.
He said: "It is a sin."
And so to the end.
Always He said: "It is a sin."
At last, I cried out:
"But I have none other."
He looked at me
With kinder eyes.
"Poor soul," he said.

———

Aye, workman, make me a dream,
A dream for my love.
Cunningly weave sunlight,
Breezes, and flowers.
Let it be of the cloth of meadows.
And—good workman—
And let there be a man walking thereon.

———

Each small gleam was a voice,
A lantern voice—
In little songs of carmine, violet, green, gold.
A chorus of colors came over the water;
The wondrous leaf-shadow no longer wavered,
No pines crooned on the hills,
The blue night was elsewhere a silence,
When the chorus of colors came over the water,
Little songs of carmine, violet, green, gold.

Small glowing pebbles
Thrown on the dark plane of evening
Sing good ballads of God
And eternity, with soul's rest.
Little priests, little holy fathers,
None can doubt the truth of your hymning,
When the marvelous chorus comes over the water,
Songs of carmine, violet, green, gold.

———

The trees in the garden rained flowers.
Children ran there joyously.
They gathered the flowers
Each to himself.
Now there were some
Who gathered great heaps—
Having opportunity and skill—
Until, behold, only chance blossoms
Remained for the feeble.
Then a little spindling tutor
Ran importantly to the father, crying:
"Pray, come hither!
"See this unjust thing in your garden!"
But when the father had surveyed,
He admonished the tutor:
"Not so, small sage!
"This thing is just.
"For, look you,
"Are not they who possess the flowers
"Stronger, bolder, shrewder
"Than they who have none?
"Why should the strong—
"The beautiful strong—
"Why should they not have the flowers?"

Upon reflection, the tutor bowed to the ground.
"My Lord," he said,
"The stars are displaced
"By this towering wisdom."

Intrigue

Thou art my love,
And thou art the peace of sundown.
When the blue shadows soothe,
And the grasses and the leaves sleep
To the song of the little brooks,
Woe is me.

Thou art my love,
And thou art a storm
That breaks black in the sky,
And, sweeping headlong,
Drenches and cowers each tree,
And at the panting end
There is no sound
Save the melancholy cry of a single owl—
Woe is me!

Thou art my love,
And thou art a tinsel thing,
And I in my play
Broke thee easily,
And from the little fragments
Arose my long sorrow—
Woe is me.

Thou art my love,
And thou art a weary violet,
Drooping from sun-caresses,
Answering mine carelessly—
Woe is me.

Thou art my love,
And thou art the ashes of other men's love,
And I bury my face in these ashes,
And I love them—
Woe is me.

Thou art my love,
And thou art the beard
On another man's face—
Woe is me.

Thou art my love,
And thou art a temple,
And in this temple is an altar,
And on this altar is my heart—
Woe is me.

Thou art my love,
And thou art a wretch.
Let these sacred love-lies choke thee,
For I am come to where I know your lies as truth
And your truth as lies—
Woe is me.

Thou art my love,
And thou art a priestess,
And in thy hand is a bloody dagger,
And my doom comes to me surely—
Woe is me.

Thou art my love,
And thou art a skull with ruby eyes,
And I love thee—
Woe is me.

Thou art my love,
And I doubt thee.
And if peace came with thy murder
Then would I murder—
Woe is me.

Thou art my love,
And thou art death,
Aye, thou art death
Black and yet black,
But I love thee,
I love thee—
Woe, welcome woe, to me.

*   *   *

Love, forgive me if I wish you grief,
For in your grief
You huddle to my breast,

And for it
Would I pay the price of your grief.

You walk among men
And all men do not surrender,
And thus I understand
That love reaches his hand
In mercy to me.

He had your picture in his room
A scurvy traitor picture,
And he smiled
—Merely a fat complacence of men who know fine
    women—
And thus I divided with him
A part of my love.

Fool, not to know that thy little shoe
Can make men weep!
—Some men weep.
I weep and I gnash,
And I love the little shoe,
The little, little shoe.

God give me medals,
God give me loud honors,
That I may strut before you, sweetheart,
And be worthy of—
The love I bear you.

Now let me crunch you
With full weight of affrighted love.
I doubted you
—I doubted you—
And in this short doubting
My love grew like a genie
For my further undoing.

Beware of my friends,
Be not in speech too civil,
For in all courtesy
My weak heart sees spectres,
Mists of desire
Arising from the lips of my chosen;
Be not civil.

The flower I gave thee once
Was incident to a stride,
A detail of a gesture,
But search those pale petals
And see engraven thereon
A record of my intention.

* * *

Ah, God, the way your little finger moved,
As you thrust a bare arm backward
And made play with your hair
And a comb, a silly gilt comb
Ah, God—that I should suffer
Because of the way a little finger moved.

*   *   *

Once I saw thee idly rocking
—Idly rocking—
And chattering girlishly to other girls,
Bell-voiced, happy,
Careless with the stout heart of unscarred womanhood,
And life to thee was all light melody.
I thought of the great storms of love as I knew it.
Torn, miserable, and ashamed of my open sorrow,
I thought of the thunders that lived in my head,
And I wish to be an ogre,
And hale and haul my beloved to a castle,
And there use the happy cruel one cruelly,
And make her mourn with my mourning.

*   *   *

Tell me why, behind thee,
I see always the shadow of another lover?
Is it real
Or is this the thrice damned memory of a better happiness?
Plague on him if he be dead,
Plague on him if he be alive—
A swinish numskull
To intrude his shade
Always between me and my peace!

*   *   *

And yet I have seen thee happy with me.
I am no fool
To poll stupidly into iron.
I have heard your quick breaths
And seen your arms writhe toward me;
At those times
—God help us—
I was impelled to be a grand knight,
And swagger and snap my fingers,
And explain my mind finely.
Oh, lost sweetheart,
I would that I had not been a grand knight.
I said: "Sweetheart."
Thou said'st: "Sweetheart."
And we preserved an admirable mimicry
Without heeding the drip of the blood
From my heart.

* * *

I heard thee laugh,
And in this merriment
I defined the measure of my pain;
I knew that I was alone,
Alone with love,
Poor shivering love,
And he, little sprite,
Came to watch with me,
And at midnight
We were like two creatures by a dead camp-fire.

*   *   *

I wonder if sometimes in the dusk,
When the brave lights that gild thy evenings
Have not yet been touched with flame,
I wonder if sometimes in the dusk
Thou rememberest a time,
A time when thou loved me
And our love was to thee thy all?
Is the memory rubbish now?
An old gown
Worn in an age of other fashions?
Woe is me, oh, lost one,
For that love is now to me
A supernal dream,
White, white, white with many suns.

*   *   *

Love met me at noonday,
—Reckless imp,
To leave his shaded nights
And brave the glare,—
And I saw him then plainly
For a bungler,
A stupid, simpering, eyeless bungler,
Breaking the hearts of brave people
As the snivelling idiot-boy cracks his bowl,
And I cursed him,
Cursed him to and fro, back and forth,

Into all the silly mazes of his mind,
But in the end
He laughed and pointed to my breast,
Where a heart still beat for thee, beloved.

* * *

I have seen thy face aflame
For love of me,
Thy fair arms go mad,
Thy lips tremble and mutter and rave.
And—surely—
This should leave a man content?
Thou lovest not me now,
But thou didst love me,
And in loving me once
Thou gavest me an eternal privilege,
For I can think of thee.

UNCOLLECTED POEMS

On the brown trail
We hear the grind of your carts
To our villages,
Laden with food
Laden with food
We know you are come to our help
But—
Why do you impress upon us
Your foreign happiness?
We know it not.
(Hark!
Carts laden with food
Laden with food)
We weep because we don't understand
But your gifts form into a yoke
The food turns into a yoke
(Hark!
Carts laden with food
Laden with food)
It is our mission to vanish
Grateful because of full mouths
Destiny—Darkness
Time understands
And ye—ye bigoted men of a moment—
—Wait—
Await your turn.

———

Rumbling, buzzing, turning, whirling Wheels,
Dizzy Wheels!
Wheels!

The Battle Hymn

All-feeling God, hear in the war-night
The rolling voices of a nation;
Through dusky billows of darkness
See the flash, the under-light, of bared swords—
—Whirling gleams like wee shells
Deep in the streams of the universe—
Bend and see a people, O, God,
A people rebuked, accursed,
By him of the many lungs
And by him of the bruised weary war-drum
(The chanting disintegrate and the two-faced eagle)
Bend and mark our steps, O, God.
Mark well, mark well, Father of the Never-Ending Circles
And if the path, the new path, lead awry
Then in the forest of the lost standards
Suffer us to grope and bleed apace
For the wisdom is Thine.
Bend and see a people, O, God,
A people applauded, acclaimed,
By him of the raw red shoulders
The manacle-marked, the thin victim
(He lies white amid the smoking cane)
—And if the path, the new path, leads straight—
Then—O, God—then bare the great bronze arm;
Swing high the blaze of the chained stars
And let them look and heed
(The chanting distintegrate and the two-faced eagle)

For we go, we go in a lunge of a long blue corps
And—to Thee we commit our lifeless sons,
The convulsed and furious dead.
(They shall be white amid the smoking cane)
For, the seas shall not bar us;
The capped mountains shall not hold us back
We shall sweep and swarm through jungle and pool,
Then let the savage one bend his high chin
To see on his breast, the sullen glow of the death-medals
For we know and we say our gift.
His prize is death, deep doom.
(He shall be white amid the smoking cane.)

———

Unwind my riddle.
Cruel as hawks the hours fly,
Wounded men seldom come home to die,
The hard waves see an arm flung high,
Scorn hits strong because of a lie,
Yet there exists a mystic tie.
Unwind my riddle.

A naked woman and a dead dwarf;
Wealth and indifference.
Poor dwarf!
Reigning with foolish kings
And dying mid bells and wine
Ending with a desperate comic palaver
While before thee and after thee
Endures the eternal clown—
—The eternal clown—
A naked woman.

———

A grey and boiling street
Alive with rickety noise.
Suddenly, a hearse,
Trailed by black carriages
Takes a deliberate way
Through this chasm of commerce;
And children look eagerly
To find the misery behind the shades.
Hired men, impatient, drive with a longing
To reach quickly the grave-side, the end of solemnity.

Yes, let us have it over.
Drive, man, drive.
Flog your sleek-hided beasts,
Gallop—gallop—gallop.
Let us finish it quickly.

Bottles and bottles and bottles
In a merry den
And the wan smiles of women
Untruthing license and joy.
Countless lights
Making oblique and confusing multiplication
In mirrors
And the light returns again to the faces.

*   *   *   *

A cellar, and a death-pale child.
A woman
Ministering commonly, degradedly,
Without manners.
A murmur and a silence
Or silence and a murmur
And then a finished silence.
The moon beams practically upon the cheap bed.

An hour, with its million trinkets of joy or pain,
Matters little in cellar or merry den
Since all is death.

The patent of a lord
And the bangle of a bandit
Make argument
Which God solves
Only after lighting more candles.

———

My cross!

Your cross?
The real cross
Is made of pounds,
Dollars or francs.
Here I bear my palms for the silly nails
To teach the lack
—The great pain of lack—
Of coin.

BIOGRAPHICAL NOTE

Stephen Crane was born on November 1, 1871, in Newark, New Jersey, the youngest of eight surviving children. His father, a Methodist pastor, died when he was eight years old; an older sister and brothers helped raise him while his mother, a temperance activist, was away from home. He attended Pennington Seminary (a boarding school) in New Jersey and Claverack College (a military academy) in New York. During the summer of 1888, he began reporting on local news for the New Jersey Coast News Bureau, run by his brother Townley, a professional journalist, continuing for several seasons. In 1890 he enrolled in the mining engineering program at Lafayette College in Easton, Pennsylvania, but neglected his coursework for baseball: "I did little work at school," he later wrote, and "confined my abilities, such as they were, to the diamond." He fared little better academically at Syracuse University, where he transferred for a term in 1891. At Syracuse, however, he published his first fiction (in the *University Herald*), along with articles and sketches in the *New York Tribune*. While reporting in New Jersey during the summer, he met and became friendly with the writer Hamlin Garland. In the fall of 1892 he moved to New York City, where he worked as a freelance journalist and began his first novel, eventually titled *Maggie: A Girl of the Streets*. Failing to find a publisher, in March 1893 he used an inheritance from his mother, who had died the previous year, to have it printed, under the pseudonym Johnston Smith. In spite of praise from Garland and William Dean Howells, it proved too controversial at first to interest booksellers or a regular publisher. He began *The Red Badge of Courage*, conceived as "a psychological portrayal of fear," around the same time; it was serialized in newspapers in December 1894. Early in 1895, he travelled west and to Mexico as a newspaper correspondent, writing feature stories, and on his return in May worked on two novels, *George's Mother* (1896) and *The Third Violet* (1897). His first collection of poetry, *The Black Riders*, was also published in May. When it finally appeared in book form in September 1895, *The Red Badge of Courage* became a best-seller. Along with his new-found fame came controversy. In September and October 1896, he was caught up in a scandal in the wake of his defense of a suspected prostitute; the police searched his apartment, and his reputation was attacked in court. He left for Cuba in November 1896 under contract as a war correspondent. En route, he met Cora Taylor, proprietress of the Hotel de Dream, a bordello in Jacksonville, Florida; she would become his common-law spouse. In January 1897, sailing to Cuba aboard the *Commodore*, his ship sank, an ordeal he barely survived and which he subsequently narrated in a famous story, "The Open Boat," written soon after. In March 1897 he traveled to Greece with Taylor, where both reported on the war with Turkey for the American press. When an armistice was declared in May, they settled in England, meeting Joseph Conrad, Henry James, H. G. Wells, and many other writers. Short of funds despite the success of *The Red Badge of Courage*, Crane wrote prolifically. In June and July 1898, he reported firsthand on the Spanish-American war, witnessing the capture of Guantánamo Bay. Diagnosed with yellow fever and malaria, and probably suffering from tuberculosis, he returned to the U.S. and finally to England in January 1899. He published a novel, *Active Service* (1899), a book of poems, *War Is Kind* (1899), and *The Monster and Other Stories* (1899), and recovered sufficiently to begin work on a new novel, *The O'Ruddy*, published posthumously in 1903. But his health continued to worsen, and he suffered several lung hemorrhages. He died of tuberculosis on June 5, 1900, shortly after his arrival at a health spa in Badenweiler, Germany.

NOTE ON THE TEXTS

This volume presents all of Stephen Crane's poetry known to be extant. It includes his two published books of poetry—*The Black Riders and Other Lines* (Boston: Copeland and Day, 1895) and *War Is Kind* (New York: Frederick A. Stokes, 1899)—along with all of the poems he left uncollected at the time of his death. The texts of Crane's books have been taken from the first printings of each. The texts of his uncollected poems have been taken from *Stephen Crane: Poems and Literary Remains* (*Works of Stephen Crane*, vol. X [Charlottesville: University Press of Virginia, 1975]), ed. Fredson Bowers, which draws its texts from manuscript or periodical sources closest to Crane's intentions, arranging them in approximate chronological order of composition. (Where available, information about the uncollected poems' dates of composition is included in the notes to the present volume.) One work, "A Prologue," has been added to the uncollected poems gathered in the Virginia edition, as a kind of prose poem or lyrical play; the text has been taken from *The Philistine* 3.2 (July 1896): 38.

Crane and his publisher, Copeland and Day, disagreed about which poems ought to be included in *The Black Riders*. In response to his initial manuscript, submitted through friends in April 1894, the firm had marked a number of poems for rejection, and also asked him to add new poems. Crane wrote back in early September. To add new poems, he explained, would be "utterly impossible." And while he agreed that some of his initial submissions were "unworthy of print," removing them from consideration, he would not yield on others: "I should absolutely refuse to have my poems printed without many of those which you just as absolutely mark 'No.' It seems to me that you cut all the ethical sense out of the book. All the anarchy, perhaps. It is the anarchy which I particularly insist upon." Ultimately, *The Black Riders* was published without seven poems which Crane had hoped to include. Of these seven, Crane later published two (with some alteration) in *War Is Kind*, and two have been published posthumously, again in somewhat different form. In the present volume, the omitted poems appear on pages 79, 94, 122, and 124. The remaining three—listed in a letter from Copeland and Day as "A god it is said / Marked a sparrow's fall," "The traveller paused in kindness," and "Should you stuff me with flowers"—are no longer known to be extant. The present volume prints the text of the May 1895 first printing of *The Black Riders*, but does not attempt to reproduce every feature of its typography. Notably, Copeland and Day decided to set Crane's poems entirely in capital letters, as part of a "severely classic" design scheme. Crane was not unhappy with the resulting effect and the responses it produced, and subsequent readers have suggested ways in which the book's typographic design enhances the poems' distinctive expressive features, but an all-capital text was never Crane's intention; when he printed poems omitted from *The Black Riders* elsewhere, he did so without such capitalization.

In March 1898, Crane wrote to his American agent, Paul Reynolds, asking him to make arrangements for a second book of poems. He suggested his friend Elbert Hubbard—publisher of *The Philistine* and founder of Roycroft Press—as a potential publisher for the collection, but by September, Reynolds had entered into contract instead with Frederick A. Stokes in New York, and Crane sent more poems, expanding the group he had originally submitted. *War Is Kind* was published in April and announced in *Publishers' Weekly* in May 1899. The text printed here is that of the 1899 first printing.

This volume presents the texts of the original printings and the scholarly edition chosen for inclusion here, but it does not attempt to reproduce nontextual features of their typographic design. The texts are presented without change, except for the correction of typographical errors. The following is a list of typographical errors corrected, cited by page and line number: 67.9, friend?; 89.28, accurséd; 106.24, flowers?.

THE BLACK RIDERS AND OTHER LINES

2.1   *The Black Riders and Other Lines*]   Crane dedicated his book "To Hamlin Garland." Garland (1860–1940), later the author of *Main-Travelled Roads* (1891), *A Son of the Middle Border* (1917), and many other books, had first met Crane in 1891; he offered the younger writer substantial encouragement and assistance in his literary career, and had helped him find a publisher for *The Black Riders*.

WAR IS KIND

77.1   "What says the sea, little shell?]   In some manuscript versions, this poem was titled "The Sea to the Pines" or "The Shell and the Pines."

79.1–2   To the maiden / The sea was a blue meadow,]   This poem was one of seven cut from Crane's original manuscript of *The Black Riders and Other Lines* by his publisher. In a letter dated October 19, 1894, detailing these omissions, the publisher gave the second line as "The sea was a laughing meadow."

92.1   A slant of sun on dull brown walls,]   In Crane's manuscript lists of his poems, this poem was titled "The Noise of the City" or "The City."

94.1   There was a man with a tongue of wood]   This poem was one of seven cut by Crane's publisher from his manuscript of *The Black Riders and Other Lines*.

UNCOLLECTED POEMS

119.1   I'd Rather Have—]   Probably written c. 1879–80.

120.1   Ah, haggard purse, why ope thy mouth] According to Crane's friend Corwin Linson, who saved the manuscript, this poem was written in December 1892.

121.1   Little birds of night] Probably written in 1894.

122.1–2   A god came to a man / And said to him thus:] This poem, probably written in 1894, was one of seven cut from Crane's original manuscript of *The Black Riders and Other Lines*. Detailing the omission, Crane's publisher gave the second line as "And spoke in this wise."

124.1   One came from the skies] This poem, probably written in 1894, was one of seven omitted by Crane's publisher from *The Black Riders and Other Lines*.

125.1   There is a grey thing that lives in the tree-tops] Probably written in 1894.

126.1   intermingled,] Probably written in 1894.

127.1   A soldier, young in years, young in ambitions] Probably written in April or May 1894. Crane included the poem in an unpublished article he submitted to the *New York Press* for Memorial Day.

128.1   A row of thick pillars] Probably written after June 1895.

129.1   Chant you loud of punishments,] Written c. 1895–96.

130.1   If you would seek a friend among men] Written c. 1895–96.

131.1   A lad and a maid at a curve in the stream] Written c. 1895–96.

132.1   A Prologue] Written c. 1896.

133.1   Legends] These poems were first published in *The Bookman* in May 1896. The title "Legends" may or may not have been Crane's own.

134.1   Oh, a rare old wine ye brewed for me] Written c. 1896.

135.1   Tell me not in joyous numbers] Written c. 1897.

136.1   When a people reach the top of a hill] This poem was first published in *The Philistine* in June 1898, under the title "Lines." It was written c. 1897.

138.1   A man adrift on a slim spar] Written c. 1897.

140.1   There exists the eternal fact of conflict] Written c. 1897.

141.1   On the brown trail] Written c. 1897.

142.1   Rumbling, buzzing, turning, whirling Wheels,] This poem was first published in *The Philistine* in December 1898 and probably written in 1898.

143.1   The Battle Hymn] A manuscript of this poem at Columbia University contains the following note: "(The ms., of above, has just been discovered in saddle-bags used by Stephen Crane during the late war with Spain.)" Written c. June–August 1898.

145.1   Unwind my riddle.] This poem was first published in the *New York Herald*, March 19, 1899, as an epigraph to Crane's story "The Clan of No-Name." Written c. October 1898.

146.1   A naked woman and a dead dwarf;] Date of composition unknown.
147.1   A grey and boiling street] Date of composition unknown.
148.1   Bottles and bottles and bottles] Date of composition unknown.
149.1   The patent of a lord] Date of composition unknown.
150.1   My cross!] Date of composition unknown.

INDEX OF TITLES
AND FIRST LINES

I'd Rather Have—

Last Christmas they gave me a sweater,
    And a nice warm suit of wool,
But I'd rather be cold and have a dog,
    To watch when I come from school.

Father gave me a bicycle,
    But that isn't much of a treat,
Unless you have a dog at your heels
    Racing away down the street.

They bought me a camping outfit,
    But a bonfire by a log
Is all the outfit I would ask,
    If I only had a dog.

They seem to think a little dog
    Is a killer of all earth's joys;
But oh, that "pesky little dog"
    Means hours of joy to the boys.

———

Ah, haggard purse, why ope thy mouth
Like a greedy urchin
I have nought wherewith to feed thee
Thy wan cheeks have ne'er been puffed
Thou knowest not the fill of pride
Why then gape at me
In fashion of a wronged one
Thou do smile wanly
And reproachest me with thine empty stomach
Thou knowest I'd sell my steps to the grave
If t'were but honestie.
Ha, leer not so,
Name me no names of wrongs committed with thee
No ghost can lay hand on thee and me
We've been too thin to do sin
What, liar? When thou was filled of gold, didst I riot?
And give thee no time to eat?
No, thou brown devil, thou art stuffed now with lies as
        with wealth,
The one gone to let in the other.

―――

Little birds of the night
Aye, they have much to tell
Perching there in rows
Blinking at me with their serious eyes
Recounting of flowers they have seen and loved
Of meadows and groves of the distance
And pale sands at the foot of the sea
And breezes that fly in the leaves.
They are vast in experience
These little birds that come in the night

———

A god came to a man
And said to him thus:
"I have an apple
"It is a glorious apple
"Aye, I swear by my ancestors
"Of the eternities before this eternity
"It is an apple that is from
"The inner thoughts of heaven's greatest.

"And this I will hang here
"And then I will adjust thee here
"Thus—you may reach it.
"And you must stifle your nostrils
"And control your hands
"And your eyes
"And sit for sixty years
"But,—leave be the apple."

The man answered in this wise:
"Oh, most interesting God
"What folly is this?
"Behold, thou hast moulded my desires
"Even as thou hast moulded the apple.

"How, then?
"Can I conquer my life
"Which is thou?

"My desires?
"Look you, foolish god
"If I thrust behind me
"Sixty white years
"I am a greater god than god
"And, then, complacent splendor,
"Thou wilt see that the golden angels
"That sing pink hymns
"Around thy throne-top
"Will be lower than my feet."

—

One came from the skies
—They said—
And with a band he bound them
A man and a woman.
Now to the man
The band was gold
And to another, iron
And to the woman, iron.
But this second man,
He took his opinion and went away
But, by heavens,
He was none too wise.

—

There is a grey thing that lives in the tree-tops
None know the horror of its sight
Save those who meet death in the wilderness
But one is enabled to see
To see branches move at its passing
To hear at times the wail of black laughter
And to come often upon mystic places
Places where the thing has just been.

—

        intermingled,
There come in wild revelling strains
Black words, stinging
That murder flowers
The horror of profane speculation.

A soldier, young in years, young in ambitions
Alive as no grey-beard is alive
Laid his heart and his hopes before duty
And went staunchly into the tempest of war.
There did the bitter red winds of battle
Swirl 'gainst his youth, beat upon his ambitions,
Drink his cool clear blood of manhood
Until at coming forth time
He was alive merely as the grey-beard is alive.
And for this—
The nation rendered to him a flower
A little thing—a flower
Aye, but yet not so little
For this flower grew in the nation's heart
A wet, soft blossom
From tears of her who loved her son
Even when the black battle rages
Made his face the face of furious urchin,
And this she cherished
And finally laid it upon the breast of him.
A little thing—this flower?
No—it was the flower of duty
That inhales black smoke-clouds
And fastens its roots in bloody sod
And yet comes forth so fair, so fragrant—
Its birth is sunlight in grimest, darkest place.

———

A row of thick pillars
Consciously bracing for the weight
Of a vanished roof
The bronze light of sunset strikes through them,
And over a floor made for slow rites.
There is no sound of singing
But, aloft, a great and terrible bird
Is watching a cur, beaten and cut,
That crawls to the cool shadows of the pillars
To die.

—

Chant you loud of punishments,
Of the twisting of the heart's poor strings
Of the crash of the lightning's fierce revenge.

Then sing I of the supple-souled men
And the strong, strong gods
That shall meet in times hereafter
And the amaze of the gods
At the strength of the men.
—The strong, strong gods—
    —And the supple-souled men—

———

If you would seek a friend among men
Remember: they are crying their wares.
If you would ask of heaven of men
Remember: they are crying their wares.
If you seek the welfare of men
Remember: they are crying their wares.
If you would bestow a curse upon men
Remember: they are crying their wares.
    Crying their wares
    Crying their wares
If you seek the attention of men
Remember:
Help them or hinder them as they cry their wares.

———

A lad and a maid at a curve in the stream
And a shine of soft silken waters
Where the moon-beams fall through a hemlock's boughs
  Oh, night dismal, night glorious.

A lad and a maid at the rail of a bridge
With two shadows adrift on the water
And the wind sings low in the grass on the shore.
  Oh, night dismal, night glorious.

A lad and a maid in a canoe,
And a paddle making silver turmoil.

A Prologue

A gloomy stage. Slender curtains at a window, centre. Before the window, a table, and upon the table, a large book, opened. A moonbeam, no wider than a sword-blade, pierces the curtains and falls upon the book.

A moment of silence.

From without, then—an adjacent room in intention— come sounds of celebration, of riotous drinking and laughter. Finally, a swift quarrel. The din and crash of a fight. A little stillness. Then a woman's scream. "Ah, my son, my son."

A moment of silence.

Curtain.

Legends

I
A man builded a bugle for the storms to blow.

The focussed winds hurled him afar.
He said that the instrument was a failure.

II
When the suicide arrived at the sky,
The people there asked him: "Why?"
He replied: "Because no one admired me."

III
A man said: "Thou tree!"
The tree answered with the same scorn: "Thou man!
Thou art greater than I only in thy possibilities."

IV
A warrior stood upon a peak and defied the stars.
A little magpie, happening there, desired the soldier's
    plume,
And so plucked it.

V
The wind that waves the blossoms
Sang, sang, sang from age to age.
The flowers were made curious by this joy.
"Oh, wind," they said, "why sing you at your labour,
While we, pink beneficiaries, sing not,
But idle, idle, idle from age to age?"

———

Oh, a rare old wine ye brewed for me
Flagons of despair
A deep deep drink of this wine of life
Flagons of despair.

Dream of riot and blood and screams
The rolling white eyes of dying men
The terrible heedless courage of babes

———

Tell me not in joyous numbers
We can make our lives sublime
By—well, at least, not by
Dabbling much in rhyme.

———

When a people reach the top of a hill
Then does God lean toward them,
Shortens tongues, lengthens arms.
A vision of their dead comes to the weak.
    The moon shall not be too old
    Before the new battalions rise
      —Blue battalions—
    The moon shall not be too old
    When the children of change shall fall
    Before the new battalions
      —The blue battalions—

Mistakes and virtues will be trampled deep
A church and a thief shall fall together
A sword will come at the bidding of the eyeless,
The God-led, turning only to beckon.
    Swinging a creed like a censer
    At the head of the new battalions
      —Blue battalions—
    March the tools of nature's impulse
    Men born of wrong, men born of right
    Men of the new battalions
      —The blue battalions—

The clang of swords is Thy wisdom
The wounded make gestures like Thy Son's
The feet of mad horses is one part,

—Aye, another is the hand of a mother on the brow of a
    son.
    Then swift as they charge through a shadow,
    The men of the new battalions
        —Blue battalions—
    God lead them high. God lead them far
    Lead them far, lead them high
    These new battalions
        —The blue battalions—.

A man adrift on a slim spar
A horizon smaller than the rim of a bottle
Tented waves rearing lashy dark points
The near whine of froth in circles.

                    God is cold.

The incessant raise and swing of the sea
And growl after growl of crest
The sinkings, green, seething, endless
The upheaval half-completed.

                    God is cold.

The seas are in the hollow of The Hand;
Oceans may be turned to a spray
Raining down through the stars
Because of a gesture of pity toward a babe.
Oceans may become grey ashes,
Die with a long moan and a roar
Amid the tumult of the fishes
And the cries of the ships,
Because The Hand beckons the mice.

A horizon smaller than a doomed assassin's cap,
Inky, surging tumults
A reeling, drunken sky and no sky
A pale hand sliding from a polished spar.

                    God is cold.

The puff of a coat imprisoning air.
A face kissing the water-death
A weary slow sway of a lost hand
And the sea, the moving sea, the sea.

God is cold.

There exists the eternal fact of conflict
And—next—a mere sense of locality.
Afterward we derive sustenance from the winds.
Afterward we grip upon this sense of locality.
Afterward, we become patriots.
The godly vice of patriotism makes us slaves,
And—let us surrender to this falsity
Let us be patriots

Then welcome us the practical men
Thrumming on a thousand drums
The practical men, God help us.
    They cry aloud to be led to war
    Ah—
    They have been poltroons on a thousand fields
    And the sacked sad city of New York is their record
Furious to face the Spaniard, these people, and crawling
        worms before their task
They name serfs and send charity in bulk to better men
They play at being free, these people of New York
Who are too well-dressed to protest against infamy.